CW01095840

OR RUE IT

BOOKS BY
FATHER PAUL O'SULLIVAN, O.P.

HOW TO BE HAPPY — HOW TO BE HOLY

ALL ABOUT THE ANGELS

AN EASY WAY TO BECOME A SAINT

THE HOLY GHOST — OUR GREATEST FRIEND

READ ME OR RUE IT

HOW TO AVOID PURGATORY

THE SECRET OF CONFESSION
Including The Wonders of Confession

READ ME
OR RUE IT

by

Father Paul O'Sullivan, O.P.
(E. D. M.)

*"It is therefore a holy and wholesome thought
to pray for the dead, that they may be loosed
from sins."* —2 Machabees 12:46

TAN BOOKS AND PUBLISHERS, INC.
Rockford, Illinois 61105

APPROVED BY HIS EMINENCE
THE CARDINAL PATRIARCH OF LISBON
March 4, 1936

First published *circa* 1936 by the former Edições do Corpo Santo, Lisbon, Portugal. Retypeset and republished in 1992 by TAN Books and Publishers, Inc. with permission of the Dominican Nuns of the Perpetual Rosary, Pius XII Monastery, Fatima, Portugal.

The type in this book is the property of TAN Books and Publishers, Inc., and may not be reproduced, in whole or in part, without written permission from the publisher. (This restriction applies to *this type*, not to quotations from the book.)

ISBN: 0-89555-458-5

Library of Congress Catalog Card No.: 92-61256

Printed and bound in the United States of America.

TAN BOOKS AND PUBLISHERS, INC.
P.O. Box 424
Rockford, Illinois 61105
1992

*This booklet will be
a revelation to many.*

APPROVAL OF HIS EMINENCE
THE CARDINAL PATRIARCH OF LISBON

Cardinal's Palace, Lisbon
March 4, 1936

We approve and recommend with all our heart the beautiful little book *Read Me or Rue It* by E. D. M. *

Although small, it is destined to do great good among Catholics, many of whom are incredibly ignorant of the great doctrine of Purgatory. As a consequence, they do little or nothing to avoid it themselves and little to help the Poor Souls who are suffering there so intensely, waiting for the Masses and prayers which should be offered for them.

It is our earnest desire that every Catholic should read this little book and spread it about as widely as possible.

✝ M. *Cardinal Patriarca*

---

* These initials used by Fr. O'Sullivan stand for *Enfant de Marie,* that is, "Child of Mary."—*Editor,*1992.

CONTENTS

Approval of His Eminence
the Cardinal Patriarch of Lisbon vi

Foreword: "Read Me or Rue It" ix

Help, Help, They Suffer So Much! xi

Purgatory xiii

1. What Is Purgatory? 1

2. Can All This Be True? 4

3. How Long Do Souls Remain in
Purgatory? 8

4. Why Pray for the Poor Souls? 15

5. How We Can Help the Holy Souls 23

6. What the Holy Souls Do for Those
Who Help Them 28

Read and Wake Up! 40

Appendix 1: The Brown Scapular 43

Appendix 2: How to Gain a Plenary
Indulgence 47

FOREWORD

"READ ME OR RUE IT."

This title is somewhat startling. Yet, Dear Reader, if you peruse this little book, you will see for yourself how well deserved it is.

The book tells us how to save ourselves and how to save others from untold suffering.

Some books are good and may be read with profit. Others are better and should be read without fail.

There are, however, books of such sterling worth by reason of the counsels they suggest, the conviction they carry with them, the urge to action they give us that it would be sheer folly not to read them.

Read Me or Rue It belongs to this class.

It is for your best interest, Dear Friend, to read it and reread it, to ponder well and deeply on its contents. You will never regret it; rather, great and poignant will be your regret if you fail to study its few but pregnant pages.

HELP, HELP,
THEY SUFFER SO MUCH!

I. We can never understand too clearly that every alms, small or great, which we give to the poor we give to God.

He accepts it and rewards it as given to Himself. Therefore, all we do for the Holy Souls, God accepts as done to Himself. It is as if we had relieved or released Him from Purgatory.

What a thought! How He will repay us!

II. As there is no hunger, no thirst, no poverty, no need, no pain, no suffering to compare with what the Souls in Purgatory endure, so there is no alms more deserving, none more pleasing to God, none more meritorious for us than the alms, the prayers, the Masses we give to the Holy Souls.

III. It is very possible that some of our own nearest and dearest ones are still suffering the excruciating pains of Purgatory and calling on us piteously for help and relief.

Is it not dreadful that we are so hardened as not to think more about them, that we are so cruel as to deliberately forget them!

For the dear Christ's sake, let us do all, but

all, we can for them.

Every Catholic ought to join the Association of the Holy Souls. (See page 23).

PURGATORY

"Have pity on me, have pity on me, at least you my friends, because the hand of the Lord hath touched me." (Job 19:21).

This is the touching prayer that the Poor Souls in Purgatory address to their friends on Earth, begging, imploring their help, in accents of the deepest anguish. Alas, many are deaf to their prayers!

It is incomprehensible how some Catholics, even those who are otherwise devout, shamefully neglect the souls in Purgatory. It would almost seem that they do not believe in Purgatory. Certain it is that their ideas on the subject are very hazy.

Days and weeks and months pass without their having a Mass said for the Holy Souls! Seldom, too, do they hear Mass for them, seldom do they pray for them, seldom do they think of them! Whilst they are enjoying the fullness of health and happiness, busy with their work, engrossed with their amusements, the Poor Souls are suffering unutterable agonies on their beds of flame.

What is the cause of this awful callousness? Ignorance: gross, inexplicable ignorance.

People do not *realize* what Purgatory is. They have no conception of its dreadful pains, and they have no idea of the long years that souls are detained in these awful fires. As a result, they take little or no care to avoid Purgatory themselves, and worse still, they cruelly neglect the Poor Souls who are already there and who depend entirely on them for help.

Dear Reader, peruse this little book with care and you will bless the day that it fell into your hands.

READ ME
OR RUE IT

Chapter 1

WHAT IS PURGATORY?

It is a prison of fire in which nearly all souls are plunged after death* and in which they suffer the intensest pain.

Here is what the great Doctors of the Church tell us of Purgatory:

So grievous is their suffering that one minute in this awful fire seems like a century.

St. Thomas Aquinas, the Prince of Theologians, says that the fire of Purgatory is equal in intensity to the fire of Hell, and that the slightest contact with it is more dreadful than all the possible sufferings of this Earth!

St. Augustine, the greatest of the Holy Doctors, teaches that to be purified of their faults previous to being admitted to Heaven, souls after death are subjected to a fire more penetrating, more dreadful than anything we can see, or feel, or conceive in this life.

"Though this fire is destined to cleanse and purify the soul," adds the Holy Doctor, "still it

---

*That is, nearly all among those souls *who are saved.*—*Editor,* 1992.

is more acute than anything we could possibly endure on Earth."

St. Cyril of Alexandria does not hesitate to say that "it would be preferable to suffer all the possible torments of Earth until the Judgment day than to pass one day in Purgatory."

Another great Saint says: "Our fire, in comparison with the fire of Purgatory, is as a refreshing breeze."

The other holy writers speak in identical terms of this awful fire.

HOW COMES IT THAT THE PAINS OF PURGATORY ARE SO SEVERE?

1. The fire we see on Earth was made by the goodness of God for our comfort and well-being. Still, when used as a torment, it is the most dreadful one we can imagine.

2. The fire of Purgatory, on the contrary, was made by the Justice of God to punish and purify us and is, therefore, incomparably more severe.

3. Our fire, at most, burns this gross body of ours, made of clay; whereas, the fire of Purgatory acts on the spiritual soul, which is unspeakably more sensitive to pain.

4. The more intense our fire is, the more speedily it destroys its victim, who therefore ceases to suffer; whereas, the fire of Purgatory inflicts the keenest, most violent pain, but never kills the soul nor lessens its sensibility.

5. Unsurpassingly severe as is the fire of Purgatory, the pain of loss or separation from God, which the souls also suffer in Purgatory, is far more severe. The soul separated from the body craves with all the intensity of its spiritual nature for God. It is consumed with an intense desire to fly to Him. Yet it is held back. No words can describe the anguish of this unsatisfied craving.

What madness, therefore, it is for intelligent beings to neglect taking every possible precaution to avoid such a dreadful fate.

It is puerile to say that it cannot be so, that we cannot understand it, that it is better not to think or speak of it. The fact remains always the same—whether we believe it, or whether we do not—that the pains of Purgatory are beyond everything we can imagine or conceive. These are the words of St. Augustine.

Chapter 2

CAN ALL THIS BE TRUE?

The existence of Purgatory is so certain that no Catholic has ever entertained a doubt of it.* It was taught from the earliest days of the Church and was accepted with undoubting faith wherever the Gospel was preached.

The doctrine is revealed in Holy Scripture and has been handed down by Tradition, taught by the infallible Church and believed by the millions and millions of faithful of all times.

Yet, as we have remarked, the ideas of many are vague and superficial on this most important subject. They are like a person who closes his eyes and walks deliberately over the edge of a yawning precipice.

They would do well to remember that the best means of lessening our term in Purgatory—or of avoiding it altogether—is to have clear ideas of it, to think well on it and to adopt the means God offers for avoiding it.

---

*The existence of Purgatory is an article of Faith which every Catholic must believe in in order to remain a Catholic and be saved.—*Editor,* 1992.

Not to think of it is *fatal*. It is nothing else than preparing for themselves a fearfully long and rigorous Purgatory.

THE POLISH PRINCE

A Polish prince who, for some political reason, had been exiled from his native country bought a beautiful castle and property in France.

Unfortunately, he had lost the Faith of his childhood and was at the time of our story engaged in writing a book against God and the existence of a future life.

Strolling one evening in his garden, he came upon a poor woman weeping bitterly. He questioned her as to the cause of her grief.

"Ah! Prince," she replied, "I am the wife of Jean [John] Marie, your former steward, who died two days ago. He was a good husband to me and a faithful servant to Your Highness. His sickness was long and I spent all our savings on the doctors, and now I have nothing left to get Masses said for his soul."

The Prince, touched by her grief, said a few kind words and, though professing no longer to believe in a future life, gave her some gold coins to have Masses said for her husband's soul.

Some time after, it was again evening, and the Prince was in his study working feverishly at his book.

He heard a loud rap at the door and without

looking up called out to the visitor to come in. The door slowly opened and a man entered and stood facing the Prince's writing table.

On glancing up, what was not the Prince's amazement to see Jean Marie, his dead steward, looking at him with a sweet smile.

"Prince," he said, "I come to thank you for the Masses you enabled my wife to have said for my soul. Thanks to the saving Blood of Christ, which was offered for me, I am now going to Heaven, but God has allowed me to come and thank you for your generous alms."

He then added impressively: "Prince, there is a God, a future life, a Heaven and a Hell."

Having said these words he disappeared.

The Prince fell upon his knees and poured forth a fervent *Credo* ("*I believe* in God . . .").

ST. ANTONINUS AND HIS FRIEND

Here is a narrative of a different kind, but not less instructive.

St. Antoninus, the illustrious Archbishop of Florence, relates that a pious gentleman had died, who was a great friend of the Dominican Convent in which the Saint resided. Many Masses and suffrages were offered for his soul.

The Saint was very much afflicted when, after the lapse of a long time, the soul of the poor gentleman appeared to him, suffering excruciating pains.

"Oh, my Dear Friend," exclaimed the Archbishop, "are you still in Purgatory, you who led such a pious and devout life?"

"Yes, and I shall remain there still for a long time," replied the poor sufferer, "for when on Earth I neglected to offer suffrages* for the souls in Purgatory. Now, God by a just judgment has applied the suffrages which have been offered for me to those souls for whom I should have prayed."

"But God, too, in His Justice, will give me all the merits of my good works when I enter Heaven; but first of all, I have to expiate my grave neglect in regard to others."

So true are the words of Our Lord: "By that measure with which you measure, it will be measured to you again."

Remember, you who read these lines, that the terrible fate of this pious gentleman will be the fate of all those who neglect to pray for and refuse to help the Holy Souls.

---

*Suffrages—prayers and good works offered up to God for the relief of the Souls in Purgatory.—*Editor,* 1992.

Chapter 3

HOW LONG DO SOULS REMAIN
IN PURGATORY?

The length of time souls are detained in Purgatory depends on:

a) the number of their faults;

b) the malice and deliberation with which these have been committed;

c) the penance done, or not done, the satisfaction made, or not made for sins during life;

d) Much, too, depends on the suffrages offered for them after death.

What can safely be said is that the time souls spend in Purgatory is, as a rule, very much longer than people commonly imagine.

We will quote a few of the many instances which are recounted in the lives and revelations of the Saints.

St. Louis Bertrand's father was an exemplary Christian, as we should naturally expect, being the father of so great a Saint. He had even wished to become a Carthusian monk until he learned that it was not God's will for him.

When he died, after long years spent in the practice of every Christian virtue, his saintly son, fully aware of the rigors of God's Justice, offered many Masses and poured forth the most fervent supplications for the soul he so dearly loved.

A vision of his father still in Purgatory forced him to intensify a hundredfold his suffrages. He added most severe penances and long fasts to his Masses and prayers. Yet eight whole years passed before he obtained the release of his father.

St. Malachy's sister was detained in Purgatory for a very long time, despite the Masses, prayers and heroic mortifications the Saint offered for her!

It was related to a holy nun in Pampluna, who had succeeded in releasing many Carmelite nuns from Purgatory, that most of these had spent there terms of from 30 to 60 years!

Carmelite nuns in Purgatory for 40, 50 and 60 years! What will it be for those living amidst the temptations of the World and with all their hundreds of weaknesses?

St. Vincent Ferrer, after the death of his sister, prayed with incredible fervor for her soul and offered many Masses for her release. She appeared to him at length and told him that had it not been for his powerful intercession with God, she should have remained an interminable time in Purgatory.

In the Dominican Order it is the rule to pray for the Master Generals by name on their anniversaries. Many of these have been dead *several hundred years!* They were men especially eminent for piety and learning. This rule would not be approved by the Church were it not necessary and prudent.

We do not mean to imply that all souls are detained equally long periods in the expiatory fires. Many have committed lesser faults and have done more penance. Therefore, their punishment will be much less severe.

Still, the instances we have quoted are very much to the point, for if these souls who enjoyed the intimacy, who saw the example and who shared in the intercession of great Saints during their lives and were aided by their most efficacious suffrages after death were yet detained for such a length of time in Purgatory, what may not happen to us who enjoy none of these wonderful privileges?

WHY SUCH LENGTHY EXPIATION?

The reasons are not difficult to find:

1. The malice of sin is very great. What appear to us small faults are in reality serious offenses against the infinite goodness of God. It is enough to see how the Saints wept over their faults.

We are weak, it may be urged. That is true, but then God offers us abundant graces to strengthen our weakness, gives us light to see the gravity of our faults, and the necessary force to conquer temptation. If we are still weak, the fault is all our own. We do not use the light and strength God so generously offers us; we do not pray, we do not receive the Sacraments as we should.

2. An eminent theologian wisely remarks that if souls are condemned to Hell *for all eternity* because of one mortal sin, it is not to be wondered at that other souls should be detained for long years in Purgatory who have committed countless deliberate venial sins, some of which are so grave that at the time of their commission the sinner scarcely knows if they are mortal or venial. Too, they may have committed many mortal sins for which they have had little sorrow and done little or no penance. The guilt has been remitted by absolution, but the pain due to the sins will have to be paid in Purgatory.

Our Lord tells us that we shall have to render an account for *each* and *every* idle word we say and that we may not leave our prison until we shall have paid the *last farthing*. (Cf. *Matt.* 5:26.)

The Saints committed few and slight sins, and still they sorrowed much and did severe penances. We commit many and grave sins, and we sorrow little and do little or no penance.

VENIAL SINS

It would be difficult to calculate the immense number of venial sins that any Catholic commits.

a) There is an infinite number of faults of self-love, selfishness; thoughts, words and acts of sensuality, too, in a hundred forms; faults of charity in thought, word and deed; laziness, vanity, jealousy, tepidity and innumerable other faults.

b) There are sins of omission which we pay so little heed to. We love God so little, yet He has a thousand claims on our love. We treat Him with coldness, indifference and base ingratitude. He died for each one of us. Do we ever thank Him as we ought? He remains day and night on the Altar, waiting for our visits, anxious to help us. How seldom we go to Him! He longs to come into our hearts in Holy Communion, and we refuse Him entrance. He offers Himself up for us on the Altar every morning at Mass and gives oceans of graces to those who assist at the Great Sacrifice. Yet many are too lazy to go to this Calvary! What an abuse of grace!

c) Our hearts are mean and hard, full of self-love. We have happy homes, splendid food, warm clothing, an abundance of all good things. Many around us live in hunger and misery, and we give them so little; whereas, we spend lavishly and needlessly on ourselves.

d) Life is given us to serve God, to save our souls. Most Christians, however, are satisfied to give God five minutes of prayer in the morning, five minutes at night! The rest of the 24 hours is given to work, rest and pleasure. Ten minutes to God, to our immortal souls, to the great work we have to do, viz., our salvation. Twenty-three hours and 50 minutes to this transitory life! Is it fair to God?

It may be alleged that our work, our rest, our sufferings are done for God!

They should be, and then our merits would be indeed great. The truth is that many scarcely ever think of God during the day. The one engrossing object of their thoughts is self. They think and labor and rest and sleep to satisfy self. God gets a very little place in their day and in their minds. This is an outrage to His loving Heart, which is ever thinking of us.

NOW TO COME TO MORTAL SINS

e) Many Christians unfortunately commit mortal sins during their lives, but though they confess them, they make no due satisfaction for them, as we have already said.

The Venerable Bede appears to be of the opinion that those who pass a great part of their lives in the commission of grave sins and confess them on their deathbed may be detained in Purgatory even until the Last Day.

St. Gertrude in her revelations states that those who have committed many grave sins and have not done due penance may not share in the ordinary suffrages of the Church for a very considerable time!

CONCLUSION

All those sins, mortal and venial, are accumulating for the 20, 30, 40, 60 years of our lives. Each and every one has to be atoned for after death.

Is it, then, any wonder that souls have to remain so long in Purgatory?

Chapter 4

WHY PRAY FOR THE POOR SOULS?

Our Lord's Great Law is that we must love one another, genuinely and sincerely. The First Great Commandment is to love God with all our heart and soul. The Second, or rather a part of the First, is to love our neighbor as ourselves. This is not a counsel or a mere wish of the Almighty. It is His Great Commandment, the very base and essence of His Law. So true is this that He takes as done to Himself what we do for our neighbor, and as refused to Himself what we refuse to our neighbor.

We read in the Gospel of St. Matthew (*Matt.* 25:34-46) the words that Christ will address to the just on Judgment Day:

34 Then shall the king say to them that shall be on his right hand: Come, ye blessed of my Father, possess you the kingdom prepared for you from the foundation of the world.

35 For I was hungry, and you gave me to eat; I was thirsty, and you gave me to drink; I was a stranger, and you took me in:

36 Naked, and you covered me: sick, and you visited me: I was in prison, and you came to me.

37 Then shall the just answer him, saying: Lord, when did we see thee hungry, and fed thee; thirsty, and gave thee drink?

38 And when did we see thee a stranger, and took thee in? or naked, and covered thee?

39 Or when did we see thee sick or in prison, and came to thee?

40 And the king answering, shall say to them: Amen I say to you, as long as you did it to one of these my least brethren, you did it to me.

41 Then he shall say to them also that shall be on his left hand: Depart from me, you cursed, into everlasting fire which was prepared for the devil and his angels.

42 For I was hungry, and you gave me not to eat: I was thirsty, and you gave me not to drink.

43 I was a stranger, and you took me not in: naked, and you covered me not: sick and in prison, and you did not visit me.

44 Then they also shall answer him, saying: Lord, when did we see thee hungry, or thirsty, or a stranger, or naked, or sick, or in prison, and did not minister to thee?

45 Then he shall answer them, saying: Amen I say to you, as long as you did it not to one of these least, neither did you do it to me.

46 And these shall go into everlasting punishment: but the just, into life everlasting.

Some Catholics seem to think that this Law has fallen into abeyance in these days of self-assertion and selfishness, when everyone thinks only of himself and his personal aggrandizement.

"It is useless to urge the Law of Love nowadays," they say, "everyone has to shift for himself, or go under."

No such thing! God's great Law is still and will ever be *in full force.* Nay, it is more than ever necessary, more than ever our duty and more than ever our own best interest.

WE ARE BOUND TO PRAY
FOR THE HOLY SOULS

We are always bound to love and help each other, but the greater the need of our neighbor, the more stringent and the more urgent this obligation is. It is not a favor that we may do or leave undone, it is our duty: we must help each other.

It would be a monstrous crime, for instance, to refuse the poor and destitute the food necessary to keep them alive. It would be appalling to refuse aid to one in direst need, to pass by and not extend a hand to save a drowning man. Not only must we help others when it is easy and convenient, but we must make every sacrifice, when need be, to succor our brother in distress.

Now, who can be in more urgent need of our charity than the souls in Purgatory? What hunger or thirst or dire sufferings on this Earth can compare to their dreadful torments? Neither the poor nor the sick nor the suffering we see around

us have any such urgent need of our succor. Yet
we find many good-hearted people who interest
themselves in every other type of suffering, but
alas, scarcely one who works for the Holy Souls!

Who can have more claim on us? Among them,
too, there may be our mothers and fathers, our
friends and near of kin.

GOD WISHES US TO HELP THEM

In any event, they are God's dearest friends.
He longs to help them; He desires most earnestly
to have them in Heaven. They can never again
offend Him, and they are destined to be with
Him for all Eternity. True, God's Justice demands
expiation of their sins, but by an amazing dis-
pensation of His Providence He places in *our
hands* the means of assisting them, He gives us
the power to relieve and even release them. Nothing pleases Him more than for us to help them.
He is as grateful to us as if we had helped
Himself.

OUR LADY WANTS US TO HELP THEM

Never did a mother of this Earth love so tenderly
a dying child, never did she strive so earnestly to
soothe its pains, as Mary seeks to console her
suffering children in Purgatory, to have them with
her in Heaven. We give her unbounded joy each
time we take a soul out of Purgatory.

THE HOLY SOULS WILL REPAY US
A THOUSAND TIMES OVER

But what shall we say of the feelings of the Holy Souls themselves? It would be utterly impossible to describe their unbounded gratitude to those who help them! Filled with an *immense* desire to repay the favors done them, they pray for their benefactors with a fervor so great, so intense, so constant that God can refuse them nothing. **St. Catherine of Bologna** says: "I received many and very great favors from the Saints, but still greater favors from the Holy Souls."

When they are finally released from their pains and enjoy the beatitude of Heaven, far from forgetting their friends on Earth, their gratitude knows no bounds. Prostrate before the Throne of God, they never cease to pray for those who helped them. By their prayers they shield their friends from the dangers and protect them from the evils that threaten them.

They will never cease these prayers until they see their benefactors safely in Heaven, and they will be forever their dearest, sincerest and best friends.

Did Catholics only know what powerful protectors they secure by helping the Holy Souls, they would not be so remiss in praying for them.

THE HOLY SOULS WILL LESSEN
OUR PURGATORY

Another great grace that they obtain for their helpers is a short and easy Purgatory, or possibly its *complete* remission!

Saint John Massias, the Dominican lay brother, had a wonderful devotion to the Souls in Purgatory. He obtained by his prayers (chiefly by the recitation of the Rosary) the liberation of *one million four hundred thousand souls!*

In return, they obtained for him the most abundant and extraordinary graces and came at the hour of his death to help and console him and accompany him to Heaven.

This fact is so certain that it was inserted by the Church in the bull of his beatification.

The learned Cardinal Baronius recounts a similar incident.

He was himself called to assist a dying gentleman. Suddenly, a host of blessed spirits appeared in the chamber of death, consoled the dying man and chased away the devils who sought, by a last desperate effort, to compass his ruin.

When asked who they were, they made answer that they were 8,000 souls whom he had released from Purgatory by his prayers and good works. They were sent by God, so they said, to take him to Heaven without his passing one moment in Purgatory.

St. Gertrude was *fiercely* tempted by the devil when she came to die. The evil spirit reserves a dangerous and subtle temptation for our last moments. As he could find no other ruse sufficiently clever with which to assail the Saint, he thought to disturb her beautiful peace of soul by suggesting that she would surely remain long years in the awful fires of Purgatory since, he reminded her, she had long ago made over all her suffrages to other souls.* But Our Blessed Lord, not content with sending His Angels and the thousands of souls she had released to assist her, came Himself in person to drive away Satan and comfort His dear Saint. He told St. Gertrude that in exchange for all she had done for the Holy Souls, He would take her straight to Heaven and would *multiply a hundredfold* all her merits.

Blessed Henry Suso, of the Dominican Order, made a compact with a fellow religious to the effect that, when one of the two died, the survivor would offer two Masses each week for his soul, and other prayers as well.

It so fell out that his companion died first,

---

*St. Gertrude had made "the Heroic Act" of Charity. (See page 26).—*Editor,* 1992.

and Blessed Henry commenced immediately to
offer the promised Masses. These he continued
to say for a long time. At last, quite sure that
the soul of his saintly friend had reached
Heaven, he ceased offering the Masses.

Great was his sorrow and consternation when
the soul of the dead brother appeared to him,
suffering intensely and chiding him for not
celebrating the promised Masses.

Blessed Henry replied with deep regret that
he had not continued the Masses, believing that
his friend must be enjoying the Beatific Vision,
but he added that he had ever remembered him
in prayer.

"O dear Brother Henry, please give me the
Masses, for it is the Precious Blood of Jesus that
I most need!" cried out the suffering soul.

Blessed Henry began anew and, with redou-
bled fervor, offered Masses and prayers for his
friend until he received absolute certitude of
his delivery.

Then it was his turn to receive graces and
blessings of all kinds from the dear brother he
had relieved, and very many times more than
he could have expected.

Chapter 5

HOW WE CAN HELP THE HOLY SOULS

I. The first means is by joining the **Association of the Holy Souls.** The conditions are easy:

a) Have your name registered in the Book of the Association.

b) Hear Mass once a week (Sunday suffices) for the Holy Souls.

c) Pray for and promote devotion to the Holy Souls.

d) Contribute once a year an offering to the Mass Fund, which enables the Association to have perpetual Masses said every month.

(If special Masses for the Holy Souls are desired, it is important to mention how many Masses you want offered.)

Those who wish to join and do not have the Association in their parish can send their name, address and annual alms to the **Association of the Holy Souls, Dominican Nuns of the Perpetual Rosary, Pius XII Monastery, Rua do Rosário 1, 2495 Fátima, Portugal.***

---

*In 1985 the Association was moved from Lisbon to Fatima and entrusted to the Dominican Nuns of the Perpetual Rosary. They combined it with their Dominican Purgatorian

This Association is approved by the Cardinal Archbishop of Lisbon.

II. A second means of helping the Holy Souls is by **having Masses offered** for them. This is certainly the most efficacious way of relieving them.

III. Those who cannot get many Masses offered, owing to the want of means, ought to **assist at as many Masses as possible** for this intention.

A young man who was earning a very modest salary told the writer: "My wife died a few years ago. I got 10 Masses said for her. I could not possibly do more, but *heard 1,000* for her dear soul."

IV. The recital of the **Rosary** (with its great indulgences) and making the **Way of the Cross** (which is also richly indulgenced) are excellent means of helping the Holy Souls.

St. John Massias, as we saw, released from Purgatory more than a million souls, chiefly by reciting the Rosary and offering its great indulgences for them.

Society, adding extra Masses. (Those who wish may enroll a departed soul in this Purgatorian Society, to receive perpetual remembrance in Holy Mass, Divine Office, Rosary Hours and other prayers. An offering should accompany such requests.)—*Editor*, 1992.

V. Another easy and efficacious way is by the constant repetition of **short indulgenced prayers*** [applying the indulgence to the Souls in Purgatory]. Many people have the custom of saying 500 or 1,000 times each day the little ejaculation, **"Sacred Heart of Jesus, I place my trust in Thee!"** or the one word, **"Jesus."** These are most consoling devotions; they bring oceans of grace to those who practice them and give immense relief to the Holy Souls.

Those who say the ejaculations 1,000 times a day gain *300,000 days* Indulgence! What a multitude of souls they can thus relieve! What will it not be at the end of a month, a year, 50 years? And if they do not say the ejaculations, what an immense number of graces and favors they shall have lost! It is quite possible—and even easy—to say these ejaculations 1,000 times a day. But if one does not say them 1,000 times, let him say them 500 or 200 times.

VI. Still another powerful prayer is:

"Eternal Father, I offer Thee the most Precious Blood of Jesus, with all the Masses being said all over the world this day, for the Souls in Purgatory."

---

* Although the Church's regulations on indulgences, including those on ejaculations, have changed, perhaps we may still hope to obtain these same indulgences from God if we ask Him for them with great confidence.—*Editor,* 1992.

Our Lord showed **St. Gertrude** a vast number of souls leaving Purgatory and going to Heaven as a result of this prayer, which the Saint was accustomed to say frequently during the day.

VII. The Heroic Act consists in offering to God in favor of the Souls in Purgatory all the works of satisfaction* we practice during life and all the suffrages that will be offered for us after death. If God rewards so abundantly the most trifling alms given to a poor man in His name, what an immense reward will He not give to those who offer *all their works of satisfaction* in life and death for the Souls He loves so dearly.

This Act does not prevent priests from offering Mass for the intentions they wish, or lay people from praying for any persons or other intentions they desire. We counsel everyone to make this act.

ALMS HELP THE HOLY SOULS

St. Martin gave half of his cloak to a poor beggar, only to find out afterwards that it was to Christ he had given it. Our Lord appeared to him and thanked him.

Blessed Jordan of the Dominican Order could never refuse to give an alms when it was asked

---

*"Satisfaction" means "making up" for sins, either on earth or in Purgatory.—*Editor*, 1992.

in the Name of God. One day he had forgotten his purse. A poor man implored an alms for the love of God. Rather than refuse him, Jordan, who was then a student, gave him a most precious cincture or "girdle" which he prized dearly. Shortly after, he entered a church and found his cincture encircling the waist of an image of Christ Crucified. He, too, had given his alms to Christ. We all give our alms to Christ.

RESOLUTION

a) Let us give all the alms we can afford;
b) Let us have said all the Masses in our power;
c) Let us hear as many more as is possible;
d) Let us offer all our pains and sufferings *for the relief of the Holy Souls.*

We shall thus deliver countless Souls from Purgatory, who will repay us ten thousand times over.

Chapter 6

WHAT THE HOLY SOULS DO FOR THOSE WHO HELP THEM

St. Alphonsus Liguori says that, although the Holy Souls cannot merit for themselves, they can obtain for us great graces. They are not, formally speaking, intercessors, as the Saints are, but through the sweet Providence of God, they can obtain for us as astounding favors and deliver us from evils, sickness and dangers of every kind.

It is beyond all doubt, as we have already said, that they repay us a thousand times for anything we do for them.

The following facts, a few hundred of which we might quote, are sufficient to show what powerful and generous friends the Holy Souls are.

HOW A GIRL FOUND HER MOTHER

A poor servant girl in France named Jeanne Marie once heard a sermon on the Holy Souls which made an indelible impression on her mind. She was deeply moved by the thought of the intense and unceasing sufferings the Poor

Souls endure, and she was horrified to see how cruelly they are neglected and forgotten by their friends on Earth.

Among other things the preacher stressed was that many souls who are in reality near to their release—one Mass might suffice to set them free—are oftentimes long detained; it may be for years, just because the last needful suffrage has been withheld or forgotten or neglected!

With her simple faith, Jeanne Marie resolved that, cost what it might, she would have a Mass said for the Poor Souls every month, especially for the soul nearest to Heaven. She earned little, and it was sometimes difficult to keep her promise, but she never failed.

On one occasion she went to Paris with her mistress and there fell ill, so that she was obliged to go to the hospital. Unfortunately, the illness proved to be a long one, and her mistress had to return home, hoping that her maid would soon rejoin her. When at last the poor servant was able to leave the hospital, all she had left of her scanty earnings was *one franc!*

What was she to do? Where to turn? Suddenly, the thought flashed across her mind that she had not had her usual monthly Mass offered for the Holy Souls. But she had only one franc! That was little enough to buy her food. Yet her confidence that the Holy Souls would not fail her triumphed. She made her way into a church and asked a priest, just about to say Mass, if he would offer it for the Holy Souls. He consented to do so, never dreaming that the modest alms offered was the only money the poor girl possessed.

At the conclusion of the Holy Sacrifice, our heroine left the church. A wave of sadness clouded her face; she felt utterly bewildered.

A young gentleman, touched by her evident distress, asked her if she was in trouble and if he could help her. She told her story briefly, and ended by saying how much she desired work.

Somehow she felt consoled at the kind way in which the young man listened to what she said, and she fully recovered her confidence.

"I am delighted beyond measure," he said, "to help you. I know a lady who is even now looking for a servant. Come with me." And so saying he led her to a house not far distant and bade her ring the bell, assuring her that she would find work.

In answer to her ring, the lady of the house herself opened the door and inquired what Jeanne Marie required. "Madam," she said, "I have been told that you are looking for a servant. I have no work and should be glad to get the position."

The lady was amazed and replied: "Who could have told you that I needed a servant? It was only a few minutes ago that I had to dismiss my maid, and that at a moment's notice. You did not meet her?"

"No, Madam. The person who informed me

that you required a servant was a young gentleman."

"Impossible!" exclaimed the lady. "No young man, in fact no one at all, could have known that I needed a servant."

"But Madam," the girl answered excitedly, pointing to a picture on the wall, "that is the young man who told me!"

"Why, child, that is my only son, who has been dead for more than a year!"

"Dead or not," asserted the girl with deep conviction in her voice, "it was he who told me to come to you, and he even led me to the door. See the scar over his eye; I would know him anywhere."

Then followed the full story of how, with her last franc, she had had Mass offered for the Holy Souls, especially for the one nearest to Heaven.

Convinced at last of the truth of what Jeanne Marie had told her, the lady received her with open arms. "Come," she said, "though not as my servant, but as my dear daughter. You have sent my darling boy to Heaven. I have no doubt that it was he who brought you to me."

HOW A POOR BOY BECAME A BISHOP, A CARDINAL, AND A SAINT

St. Peter Damian lost both father and mother shortly after his birth. One of his brothers adopted him, but treated him with unnatural harshness, forcing him to work hard and giving him poor food and scanty clothing.

One day Peter found a silver piece, which represented to him a small fortune. A friend told him that he could conscientiously use it for himself, as the owner could not be found.

The only difficulty Peter had was to choose what it was he most needed, for he was in sore need of many things.

While turning the matter over in his young mind, it struck him that he could do a still better thing, viz., have a Mass said for the Holy Souls in Purgatory, especially for the souls of his dear parents. At the cost of a great sacrifice, he put this thought into effect and had the Mass offered.

The Holy Souls repaid his sacrifice most generously. From that day forward a complete change became noticeable in his fortunes.

His eldest brother called at the house where he lived and, horrified at the brutal hardships the little fellow was subjected to, arranged that he be handed over to his own care. He clad him and fed him as his own child, and educated and cared for him most affectionately. Blessing followed upon blessing. Peter's wonderful talents became known, and he was rapidly promoted to the priesthood; sometime after he was raised to the episcopacy and, finally, created Cardinal. Miracles attested his great sanctity, so that after death he was canonized and made a Doctor of the Church.

These wonderful graces came to him after that one Mass said for the Holy Souls.

AN ADVENTURE IN THE APENNINES

A group of priests was called to Rome to treat of a grave business matter. They were bearers of important documents, and a large sum of money was entrusted to them for the Holy Father. Aware that the Apennines, over which they had to pass, were infested by daring bandits, they chose a trusty driver. There was no tunnel through the mountains nor train in those days.

They placed themselves under the protection of the Holy Souls and decided to say a *De Profundis* every hour for them.

When right in the heart of the mountains, the driver gave the alarm and at the same time lashed the horses into a furious gallop. Looking around, the priests saw fierce bandits at each side of the road with rifles aimed, ready to fire. They were amazed that no shot rang out. They were completely at the mercy of the bandits.

After an hour's headlong flight, the driver stopped and, looking at the priests, said: "I cannot understand how we escaped. These desperadoes never spare anyone."

The Fathers were convinced that they owed their safety to the Holy Souls, a fact that was afterwards confirmed beyond doubt.

When their business was concluded in Rome,

one of their number was detained in the Eternal City, where he was appointed chaplain to a prison. Not long after, one of the fiercest brigands in Italy was captured, condemned to death for a long series of murders and was awaiting execution in this prison.

Anxious to gain his confidence, the chaplain told him of several adventures he himself had had and, finally, of his recent escape in the Apennines. The criminal manifested the greatest interest in the story. When it was ended, he exclaimed: "I was the leader of that band! We thought that you had money and we determined to rob and murder you. An invisible force prevented each and all of us from firing, as we assuredly would have done had we been able."

The chaplain then told the brigand of how they had placed themselves under the protection of the Holy Souls, and that they ascribed their deliverance to their protection.

The bandit found no difficulty in believing it. In fact, it made his conversion more easy. He died full of repentance.

HOW POPE PIUS IX CURED A BAD MEMORY

The venerable Pontiff, Pius IX, appointed a holy and prudent religious named **Padre Tomaso** to be bishop of a diocese. The priest, alarmed at the responsibility put upon him, begged earnestly to be excused.

His protests were in vain. The Holy Father knew his merits.

Overcome with apprehension, the humble religious solicited an audience with the Pope, who received him most graciously. Once more he pleaded earnestly to be excused, but the Pope was immovable.

As a last recourse, Padre Tomaso told the Holy Father that he had a very bad memory, which would naturally prove to be a grave impediment in the high office put upon him.

Pius IX answered with a smile: "Your diocese is very small in comparison with the Universal Church, which I carry on my shoulders. Your cares will be very light in comparison with mine.

"I, too, suffered from a grave defect of memory, but I promised to say a fervent prayer daily for the Holy Souls, who, in return, have obtained for me an excellent memory. Do you likewise, Dear Father, and you will have cause to rejoice."

THE MORE WE GIVE, THE MORE WE GET

A businessman in Boston joined the Association of the Holy Souls and gave a large sum of money annually that prayers and Masses might be said for them.

The Director of the Association was surprised at the gentleman's generosity, for he knew that he was not a rich man. He asked kindly one day if the alms he so generously gave were his own offering or donations which he had gathered from others.

"What I offer, Dear Fathers," the gentleman said, "is my own offering. Be not alarmed. I am not a very rich man, and you may think that I give more than I am able to do. It is not so, for far from losing by my charity, the Holy Souls see to it that I gain considerably more than I give. They are second to none in generosity."

THE PRINTER OF COLOGNE

The celebrated printer of Cologne, **William Freyssen,** gives us the following account of how his child and wife were restored to health by the Holy Souls.

William Freyssen got the order to print a little work on Purgatory. When he was correcting the proofs, his attention was caught by the facts narrated in the book. He learned for the first time what wonders the Holy Souls can work for their friends.

Just at that time his son fell grievously ill, and soon the case became desperate. Remembering what he had read about the power of the Holy Souls, Freyssen at once promised to spread, at his own expense, a hundred copies of the book which his firm was printing. To make the promise more solemn, he went to the church and there made his vow. At once a sense of peace and confidence filled his soul. On his return home, the boy, who had been unable to swallow a drop of water, asked for food. Next day he was out of danger and soon completely cured.

At once, Freyssen ordered the books on Purgatory to be distributed, feeling sure that it was the best way to obtain help for the suffering souls, by interesting a hundred people in them. No one who knows what the Poor Souls suffer can refuse to pray for them.

Time passed, and a new sorrow fell to the share of the printer. This time his dear wife was stricken down and, despite every care, grew daily worse. She lost the use of her mind and was almost completely paralyzed, so that the doctor gave up all hope.

The husband, bethinking him of what the Holy Souls had done for his boy, again ran to the church and promised to distribute 200 of the books on Purgatory, begging in exchange the urgent succor of the Holy Souls.

Wonderful to relate, the mental aberration ceased, his wife's mind became normal, and she recovered the use of her limbs and of her tongue. In a short time she was perfectly restored to health.

THE CURE OF A CANCER

D. Joana de Menezes thus tells of her cure: She was suffering severely from a cancerous growth in the leg and was plunged in grief.

Remembering what she had heard of the power of the Souls in Purgatory, she resolved to place all her confidence in them and had nine Masses offered for them. She promised, moreover, to publish news of her cure if it were granted.

Gradually the swelling went down, and the tumor and cancer disappeared.

AN ESCAPE FROM BRIGANDS

Father Louis Manaci, a zealous missionary, had great devotion to the Souls in Purgatory. He found himself obliged to set out on a dangerous journey, but confidently asked the Holy Souls to protect him in the dangers that he was likely to meet with. His road lay through a vast desert, which he knew to be infested with brigands. While plodding along, saying the Rosary for the Holy Souls, what was not his surprise, on looking around, but to find himself surrounded by a bodyguard, as it were, of blessed spirits. Soon he discovered the reason. He had fallen into an ambuscade of brigands, but the Holy Souls at once surrounded him and drove off the miscreants, who sought his life. The Holy Souls did not abandon him until he was well out of danger.

A RETURN TO LIFE

The Prior of Cirfontaines gives us his story: "A young man of my parish fell dangerously ill with a typhoid fever. His parents were overcome with grief and asked me to recommend him to the prayers of the members of the Association of the Holy Souls.

"It was Saturday. The boy was at death's door. The doctors had had recourse to every remedy. All in vain. They could think of nothing more. They were in despair.

"I was the only one who had hope. I knew the power of the Holy Souls, for I had already seen what they could do.

"On Sunday I begged the Associates of the Holy Souls to pray fervently for our sick friend.

"On Monday the danger passed. The boy was cured."

READ AND WAKE UP!

"In my long life," writes a priest, "I have noticed with amazement how few Catholics give *generously* to the poor and needy, notwithstanding what Our Blessed Lord commands them to do.

"I have also remarked that *some* Catholics are, indeed, very generous and good. Some care for the poor, others look after the sick. Lepers, consumptives, cancer patients, the mentally deficient, all have their friends. Some prefer to help the young, the hearts of others go out to the old. All the various classes of the poor and needy find champions—though, as I have said, these are not nearly as many and generous as they should be.

"The strangest thing of all is that I have never met one man or woman who has dedicated himself or herself *entirely,* whole-heartedly, to the greatest of all charities, to the greatest of all the needy—viz., the Holy Souls in Purgatory.

"There may be a few who do so, but in my *long* and *very varied* experience, I have never met any."

Alas, the words of this good priest are only too true!

We appeal to those who have not as yet dedicated themselves to any particular form of charity to dedicate all their energies to the Holy Souls. Let them do what they can *personally,* and also induce others to help.

The best way is to practice the counsels contained in this booklet and to spread about hundreds of copies of this inexpensive little book and thus make hundreds of friends for the Holy Souls. For who can read it and refuse to help them?

HOW TO AVOID PURGATORY
by Fr. Paul O'Sullivan, O.P.
(E. D. M.)

This precious little booklet should be read by everyone desirous of a happy death and of avoiding the awful fires of Purgatory.

The booklet is eminently practical, and the means it suggests for avoiding Purgatory are easy and within the reach of everyone.

Many—we daresay *most*—souls who are saved go to Purgatory after death, simply because they have never heard how easy it is to avoid these dreadful fires, or at least to lessen notably the time and lessen the pains which otherwise will be so long and so intense. This beautiful booklet, *How to Avoid Purgatory*, makes this very clear.

Dear Reader, make sure to read it.

Appendix 1

THE BROWN SCAPULAR

(The following official information was obtained from the National Scapular Center, Darien, Illinois, May 9, 1986.)

Two wonderful promises of Our Lady of Mount Carmel are available to those who have been enrolled in the Brown Scapular.

The great promise of the Blessed Virgin Mary, given to St. Simon Stock on July 16, 1251, is as follows: *"Whoever dies wearing this scapular shall not suffer eternal fire."*

Our Lady's second Scapular Promise, known as the **Sabbatine Privilege** (the word "Sabbatine" meaning "Saturday"), was given by the Blessed Virgin Mary to Pope John XXII in the year 1322 and is as follows: *"I, the Mother of Grace, shall descend on the Saturday after their death, and whomsoever I shall find in Purgatory, I shall free."*

There are three conditions for obtaining this privilege: 1) the wearing of the Brown Scapular; 2) the practice of chastity according to one's state of life; 3) the daily recitation of the Little Office of the Blessed Virgin Mary.

Those who cannot read can abstain from meat

on Wednesdays and Saturdays instead of reciting the Little Office. Also, any priest who has diocesan faculties (this includes most priests) has the additional faculty to commute (change) the third requirement into another pious work—for example, the daily Rosary.

Because of the greatness of the Sabbatine privilege, the Carmelite Order suggests that the third requirement not be commuted into anything less than the daily recitation of seven Our Fathers, seven Hail Marys, and seven Glory Be to the Fathers.

ENROLLMENT IN THE BROWN SCAPULAR
Scapular Ritual for Priests

Blessing and clothing with the Scapular of the Blessed Virgin Mary of Mt. Carmel enrolls the individual in the Scapular Confraternity (Confraternity of Our Lady of Mt. Carmel), a very large prayer organization. Scapular wearers share in the daily prayers of the Carmelite Order and the worldwide good works of the members of the Scapular Confraternity.

The ceremony of investing or "enrollment" in the Scapular and Confraternity is often performed after the reception of First Holy Communion. The following formula is used by the priest. *(This enrollment Ritual was obtained from the National Scapular Center, Darien, Illinois, 1990.)*

THE SHORT FORMULA OF
BLESSING AND ENROLLMENT

Priest: Show us, O Lord, Thy mercy.
All: And grant us Thy salvation.

Priest: O Lord, hear my prayer.

All: And let my cry come unto Thee.

Priest: The Lord be with thee.

All: And with thy spirit.

Priest: Let us pray:

All: O Lord Jesus Christ, Saviour of mankind, by Thy right hand sanctify † these Scapulars which Thy servants will devoutly wear for the love of Thee and of Thy Mother, the Blessed Virgin Mary of Mt. Carmel; so that by her intercession, they may be protected from the wickedness of the enemy and may persevere in Thy grace until death, Who livest and reignest forever and ever.

The priest now sprinkles the Scapulars with Holy Water, after which he places one on each person, saying:

Priest: Receive this blessed Scapular, and ask the Most Holy Virgin that, by her merits, it may be worn with no stain of sin and may protect you from all harm and bring you into everlasting life.

All: Amen.

Priest: By the power granted to me, I admit you to a share in all the spiritual works performed, with the merciful help of Jesus Christ, by the Religious of Mount Carmel, in the Name of the Father, and of the Son † and of the Holy Spirit.

All: Amen.

Priest: May Almighty God,

All: Creator of Heaven and earth, bless † those whom He has been pleased to receive into the Confraternity of the Blessed Virgin Mary of Mount Carmel. We beg her to crush the head of the Ancient Serpent in the hour of their death, and, in the end, to obtain for them a palm and the crown of Thine everlasting inheritance. Through Christ Our Lord. Amen.

The priest now sprinkles those enrolled with Holy Water.

Appendix 2

HOW TO GAIN
A PLENARY INDULGENCE

(The following information is taken from New Regulations on Indulgences. *Imprimatur:* ✠ *Aloysius J. Wycislo, D.D., Green Bay, Wisconsin, February 5, 1969.)*

An indulgence is the remission of temporal punishment due for sins that have already been forgiven. A *partial indulgence* remits part of the temporal punishment due; a *Plenary Indulgence* remits all one's temporal punishment. Only one Plenary Indulgence can be gained per day (except in danger of death). Both partial and Plenary Indulgences can always be offered for the Poor Souls in Purgatory.

There are many prayers and works of piety to which a **Plenary Indulgence** is attached, but these four are worthy of special mention:

1. Making a visit to the Blessed Sacrament to adore It for at least one half hour.

2. Spending at least one half hour reading Sacred Scripture, as spiritual reading, with the veneration due to the Word of God.

47

3. Making the Way of the Cross. (This includes walking from Station to Station; in a group, at least the leader must move from Station to Station.) No specific prayers are required, but it must at least include devout meditation on the Passion and Death of Our Lord.

4. Recitation of the Rosary (of at least 5 decades), with devout meditation on the Mysteries in addition to the vocal recitation, in a church, family group, religious community or some pious association.

In addition to performing the specified work, these three conditions are required:

1. Confession (within several days suffices);
2. Holy Communion;
3. prayer for the Holy Father's intentions (one Our Father and one Hail Mary suffice).

In addition, a person must be free from all attachment to sin, even venial sin. If one tries to gain a Plenary Indulgence but fails to fulfill all of the conditions, he obtains a partial indulgence.